"As a lover of words, and most particularly God's Word... with
Lauren Crews's new book *Strengt*... ...l of
thirty-one days, the reader journ... ...nce
found in Proverbs 31. Taking us ba... ...ge,
Crews develops a new image of thi... ...er
created by the most powerful God... ...we

discover a new word that points us to a vivid characteristic of women on a
kingdom mission. I'm glad the entries were short because they provide much
to ponder (and reading the companion book *Strength of a Woman* is a good
way to expand understanding of these concepts). If you think you already know
what the Proverbs 31 Woman looks like, I challenge you to explore this amazing
Hebrew poetry and embrace your own identity as *eishet chayil*—strong woman!"
—Lucinda Secrest McDowell,
author of *Soul Strong* and *Life-Giving Choices*

"With grace and skill, Lauren Crews uncovers the truth of Proverbs 31 like no
other author I've read. In short, digestible bites, my soul has been fed with the
eternal truth of Christ's love for women rather than the traditional teaching
of what a good wife and mother should do. I *like* the Proverbs 31 Woman
now! *Strength of a Woman Devotional* is brilliantly written and will help heal
women's hearts for years to come. Every woman needs to read it."
—Andy Lee, author of *A Mary Like Me: Flawed Yet Called*

"In these days when identity for women has been marred and marginalized,
this book and devotional from Lauren Crews brings to light the ancient
hidden meaning of the Proverbs 31 Woman. Hidden in the Hebrew language
and placed into its poetic context, Lauren brings honor, strength, and praise
from this Proverb to the women of today. Be refreshed in its reading to clothe
yourself in your true biblical identity!"
—Kathi Smith, senior editor of *Healing Line* magazine,
Christian Healing Ministries

Other books by Lauren Crews

Strength of a Woman: Why You Are Proverbs 31

LAUREN CREWS

Strength
of a
Woman
Devotional

31 DAYS TO CELEBRATING
YOUR PLACE IN PROVERBS 31

ASCENDER
BOOKS
An Imprint of Iron Stream Media

BIRMINGHAM, ALABAMA

Ascender Books
100 Missionary Ridge
Birmingham, AL 35242
Ascender Books is an imprint of Iron Stream Media
IronStreamMedia.com

All Scripture quotations, unless otherwise indicated, are taken from the New American
Standard Bible®, Copyright © 1960, 1962, 1963, 1968, 1971, 1972, 1973, 1975, 1977,
1995 by The Lockman Foundation Used by permission.

Author is represented by the literary agency of Credo Communications, LLC, Grand
Rapids, Michigan, www.credocommunication.net.

ISBN-13: 978-1-56309-344-9
Ebook ISBN: 978-1-56309-348-7

1 2 3 4 5—24 23 22 21 20

To Sarah-Kate, Lindsey, and Niki.
My constant prayer is that you will be women
of strength drawn from Jesus, who is the author
and perfecter of our faith and the only one who has
the final word on our value.

CONTENTS

This book's journey was long and winding. I would like to thank my husband for his steadfast walk with me during this process of learning. Thank you to the ladies who trusted me with their stories. You are incredible women of strength, and your stories will comfort and encourage many. To my Bible study partners, writing coaches, and editors, thank you for challenging my words and refining my work. My deepest prayer has been that every word will honor none other than Christ, my source of perfect strength.

What if there is more to Proverbs 31?

Most women have a love-hate relationship with the Proverbs 31 Woman. On one hand, she is godly and deserving of admiration and respect for her actions and skills. On the other hand, her near perfection is held over our heads, and she feels like an unobtainable standard. I'm tempted to skip over this Bible passage, thinking it doesn't apply to me, especially today.

Would it surprise you to learn the passage has a military theme? It also discusses the actions of a priest. As an acrostic poem, it features the Hebrew alphabet, or *alef-bet*. The passage was—and still is—used as a song to celebrate the strength of women and recognizes our honor and value.

Ancient Hebrew assigned each letter of the alphabet a word picture that represents a basic meaning of the letter and builds a related understanding. Acrostic poems are used throughout the Old Testament to help with memorization. The letter's picture, with its related meaning, acts as a memory trigger. When we read Proverbs 31:10–31 through twenty-first century eyes, with no knowledge of the Hebrew alphabet within it, we can miss the word play, the puns, and the figurative language the Israelites experienced. Much of the meaning is—literally—lost in translation.

Through this thirty-one-day devotional, we will encounter the twenty-two letters of the Hebrew alphabet. We will also look closely at the Hebrew meaning of words and themes contained in the Proverbs 31 verses and discover deeper insights. The passage primarily relates to a married woman, but all women, single, married, divorced, or widowed, can apply the lessons behind each letter to their lives. The Proverbs 31 Woman is no longer an unattainable standard. Instead, she becomes a remarkable example of strength, a prayer warrior, a watchman, and a leader.

I'm excited for you to join me as we explore this rich passage and come to truly understand the strength of this woman—from A to Z. I hope you can tuck away any preconceived ideas about the Proverbs 31 Woman and gird yourself as she does—in the strength of a relationship with Jesus. Meditate on the letters, verses, and word studies. Allow the Holy Spirit to encourage you in your relationship with Jesus Christ.

ALEF

An excellent wife, who can find?
For her worth is far above jewels. —Proverbs 31:10

After months of planning, my wedding finally arrived. With all the details reviewed and everything in place, I had a few short moments to take a deep breath. I collected myself and made a final check in the mirror. Fear and doubt took advantage of the quiet and raised their ugly heads.

Will I be a good wife? Will he love me forever . . . and always? Will I meet his expectations? I've shared some of my past discretions, but if he knew everything . . . Shame completed the trio, and my anxiety brewed.

"Yes. He chose me!" I remembered the words of my pastor from the rehearsal last night. "And the two shall become one." They felt like a soothing balm.

We will be a team. We will draw on each other's strength and work together.

Taking a deep breath, I made a few minor adjustments to my dress and picked up my bouquet. "Here we go." Exhaling slowly, I watch the door opened and took my first steps toward becoming his wife.

Alef – the Ox

Proverbs 31:10, in Hebrew, begins with a powerful phrase, *Ishsha chayil*, woman of strength. "Woman," אִשָּׁה, begins with the letter *alef*, which is

1

assigned the word picture of an ox. In biblical times, oxen were yoked together, drew on each other's strength, and worked as a team. The word *chayil* is used more than 240 times in the Bible, usually as a reference to an army or military warriors. Only twice it speaks to the strength of a woman, here in Proverbs and once in the Book of Ruth when she too is described as a woman of excellence.

If you have put your faith in Jesus Christ, you are His bride. Jesus seeks a relationship with you. You are worth pursuing, you are valuable to Him, and—like the brides of ancient times—He paid the price for you (1 Corinthians 6:20). Through an inspired author, God describes you in Proverbs 31 as a strong woman of great value who is worth searching for.

You may feel as though you work like an ox, and you may be tired and stressed. *Alef* is your encouragement to first seek a relationship with Christ and yoke yourself to Him so you can draw on His strength. This is the only way we can truly be women of strength.

Pause and Reflect

1. Strength comes in many forms: spiritual, physical, and strength of character. What strength can I offer others?

_____

_____

_____

_____

2. Who am I primarily yoked to for strength and leadership?

_____

_____

_____

_____

3. How can I strengthen this team?

_____

_____

_____

_____

Praying the *Alef-Bet*

Lord, like *alef,* You are the beginning, and nothing is before You. Jesus, I pray I will yoke myself to You and be wholly united with You. I pray Your Holy Spirit will strengthen me as I partner with You and place You first in my life. Amen.

ב

BET

The heart of her husband trusts in her,
and he will have no lack of gain. —Proverbs 31:11

Their appointment was coming to an end, but by the grace of God their marriage wasn't. Six months of counseling had repaired years of damage and provided them with a plan to implement if the warning signs reappeared.

Samantha looked at her husband. Her love for him, that once seemed elusive and dying, overwhelmed her. "We are going to make it." She smiled.

He returned her smile. "You've shown me you mean business and are willing to work hard to keep our marriage on track. So am I. That goes a long way toward rebuilding trust."

She squeezed his hand. Six months ago, Samantha didn't think they would make it to this place. "I was positive you would leave me."

He returned her squeeze and added, "I'm not perfect either, and if Jesus forgives our sin, I must be willing to do the same. You have my heart."

Bet—the House

The second letter of the Hebrew alphabet is *bet*, which begins verse 11. The letter is used in the words *heart* and *trust* in this verse. The word picture of *bet* is a *house*. This makes sense as we follow the poem. After a husband and wife are yoked together, they establish a home.

Hebrew letters are also assigned a numeric value, and bet's is two, the first number that can be divided. If a home doesn't have trust, division can gain a foothold. Our homes can be a safe place where trust resides. By yoking ourselves to Jesus and drawing on His strength, trust grows as He becomes the heart of our home. Our homes will lack no gain. Like *strength* in the last verse, *gain* in this verse is another reference to the military theme in this passage. Gain refers to the spoils of war, the added bonus of a victorious life.

In God's heart, you have value, He trusts in you, and you can rest in Him. You can trust Jesus to walk with you through the most challenging seasons in your life and celebrate your victories.

Pause and Reflect

1. What have I done to make Jesus the heart of my home?

2. What is one change I can make to deepen my trust in Jesus?

3. (If you are married) What is one change I can make to deepen my
    husband's trust?

_____

_____

_____

_____

_____

Praying the *Alef-Bet*

Lord, You reside in my heart. Whether my home is at peace or in chaos,
I desire to create a home that has an environment of trust and becomes
a blessing of encouragement. Lord, help me trust You in all I do so I
can enjoy the gains of a victorious life with You. Amen.

GIMEL

She does him good and not evil all the days of her life.
—Proverbs 31:12

The simmering disagreement was finally to the point of boiling over. It seemed no matter how Juana tried to explain her feelings, this gentleman just didn't get it and wouldn't accept her. To make matters worse, she was sure her race and being a woman was the foundation of this growing wall.

"He is so wrong!" As the words escaped her mouth, she felt a tinge of regret. She realized the power of her words and how deeply they impact others. A softness nudged her spirit as a reminder of her commitment and responsibility as a leader. That wedge would not hold the same power. She had to seek God's guidance in prayer first and ask Him to lift this burden.

Lord, give me a spirit of gentleness as I talk to those I influence. I pray they receive my words as kindness. I am weary from carrying this burden. Help me carry the load, and help him to understand how I want to be a benefit for them as I serve You.

Gimel—the Camel

Proverbs 31:12 begins with the Hebrew word *benefit*, which begins with the letter *gimel*, the word picture of a camel. Camels are known for their ability to travel desolate, dry lands and assist weary travelers by carrying their heavy burdens.

As Proverbs 31:12 states, we can be this same type of benefit for our family and anyone we serve. When we follow the poem's outline, we see we are to first yoke ourselves to God's strength and establish a home reflecting our trust in Him. Then we can receive the benefit of God's support. We, in turn, are strengthened by the Holy Spirit and extend to others our uplifting support.

Strong woman, you are called to be a benefit because of the benefit you first received from Christ. Yes, you will blow it and fail at times, but let Proverbs 31:10–12 encourage you. God is giving you His blueprint of strength so it can be said of you, "She does him good and not evil all the days of her life." You *can* do this.

Pause and Reflect

1. What burdens do I carry that can be eased by God's enduring strength?

_____

_____

_____

_____

2. How am I a benefit for others? What support do I provide?

_____

_____

_____

_____

Praying the *Alef-Bet*

Lord, thank You for bearing the burden of my sin. Your strength is a refreshing benefit when I face the dry and weary times in life. Help me extend the same goodness to others. Amen.

DALET

She looks for wool and flax and works with her hands in delight.
—Proverbs 31:13

Here she was again, left behind to clean up after everyone. "They have employees to do this," Rebekah grumbled, "and somehow it's always my job. I don't even want to be here. God, You told me to come here. You told me this was like a mission field. Well, all I see is them taking advantage of me, and certainly not for the skill I can provide."

Rebekah sensed His response to her cry. *Do not be conformed to this world but be transformed. Possess the land I promised and follow Me.*

She sighed. She knew He was right. Living a life set apart for Christ can be hard. It is so tempting to be lured into a worldly response or, worse, make a bad choice in front of someone waiting to find fault in her. *Yes, Lord. I see this as a door of opportunity. Help me walk the path You've put before me.*

Dalet—the Door

Dalet's written image resembles an animal skin hanging from the lintel, a home's entrance. *Dalet's* word picture is a door. Through this door, life's path is revealed, and the world is wide open for us.

Proverbs 31:13 begins with the Hebrew word דרש, *darash,* which means to search and seek with diligence, with all your heart as though searching for your most important possession. The items the Proverbs woman is seeking may be a reminder of how the nation of Israel was to live in the Promised Land. They were to pursue Jehovah with all their heart but remain set apart from other nations.

Wool and flax reference the priestly garments used in Israel's worship and were not to be interwoven (Deuteronomy 22:11). After ceremonial washing, the priests put on garments made of linen, which symbolized their cleanliness (Leviticus 6:10). Wearing linen implied Israel's priests were different and separated from the surrounding culture.

As a woman of strength leaves the door to her house and faces God's world, she must choose to live a life set apart for God, separated from the world. This does not mean a life of isolation, cocooned with like-minded friends but rather means one that reflects the cleansing power of God's grace and mercy in a fallen world.

God presents us with doors of opportunities and decisions every day. Our response may be the difference between someone else walking through a door of relationship with Christ or slamming it shut in His face. Strong woman, you are the welcome mat reminder for others of how godly women face the world. Seek Him, and invite others to join you.

Pause and Reflect

1. How easily do I recognize the doors of decision and opportunity God places before me?

_____

_____

_____

_____

_____

2. What is one thing I can do to ensure others recognize, like Old Testament priests, that I live a life set apart for Christ?

_____

_____

_____

_____

_____

Praying the *Alef-Bet*

Lord, Your Word encourages me to reflect You and not this world. May the doors I face in life lead me to opportunities to seek You rather than the temporary lull of anything the world offers. I dedicate my life to You, and I ask Your Holy Spirit to transform my thinking so I do not become conformed to this world. Amen.

HEI

She is like merchant ships; she brings her food from afar.
—Proverbs 31:14

J oy joined her son as he finished his prayer, "Amen. Now go to sleep, little man. You have had a big day." She gave him a peck on the nose, snuggly tucked him in, and left him to dream of floating paper boats and chasing frogs.

This home was a gift, right down to the creek in the back yard. The Lord honored their prayers, and it bolstered their faith. They navigated such loss and pain getting here, but through it all, Joy remained faithful and listened for God's voice to direct her every move. Looking out her window, she watched the leaves flutter to the ground and the bushes rustle as a gentle wind swept through her backyard.

That's You, Lord. You hold the power of a hurricane, but you choose to move us with the quiet caress of a breeze. She inhaled deeply and smiled.

Hei—the Window

Hei's word picture is a window, which is due to the fact the top left corner of the letter looks like a window and serves as a reminder of God's grace. When we recognize the devastating effect of our sin, God leaves a window open through which we can always repent and return to Him. This is the aspect of *hei* we will discuss today. Tomorrow, we will discuss another aspect.

Hei is often a reference to the Spirit or the breath of God. Psalm 33:6 declares the heavens came into being by the breath of God. Therefore *hei* also relates to the air. Consider this: When we look at the world through an open window, we see the evidence of God's presence as the air rustles the tree leaves. That is *hei*.

Like the holy name of God, *Yahweh*, *hei* is pronounced with only your breath and no sound from your throat. Isn't it humbling to know every breath you take speaks the name *Yahweh*? Try it. Breathe in *ya*, breathe out *weh*.

God's breath, His Spirit, is our link to Proverbs 31:14. Prevailing winds filled the sails of ancient ships and moved them along on their journey to exotic ports. Like these ships of long ago, a woman of strength is propelled and directed by the breath of God, His Holy Spirit. She's willing to go the distance for her loved ones, but she must be sensitive to God's directions. Those nudges from the Holy Spirit indicate her course. They may be a promise of smooth sailing or the warning of a brewing storm.

Pause and Reflect

1. How do I respond when I sense the Holy Spirit directing me?

_____

_____

_____

_____

2. Whether I am facing a storm in life or smooth sailing, how often do I check my course through God's Word? What prompts me to do so?

_____

_____

_____

_____

Praying the *Alef-Bet*

Lord, Your very breath gives me life. Father, I pray I will remain sensitive to Your leadings. Spirit of God, I depend on You to speak to me and redirect me if I am off course. Amen.

HEI

"Your name shall be Abraham; for I have made you the father
of a multitude of nations." . . . Then God said to Abraham,
"As for Sarai your wife, you shall not call her name Sarai,
but Sarah shall be her name." —Genesis 17:5, 15

Abram and Sarai left home on a promise, but their souls felt as desolate as the land they traveled. Although the famine was severe, their greatest hunger was for the presence of this God who whispered the promise of a new beginning. *This* God was different. This God was personal and breathed new life into them and left them with a sign of His continuous guidance.

Hei—Behold

Yesterday we learned *hei* represented a window and the breath of God. Today we will explore *hei's* additional meaning of behold. We often look out a window to behold the evidence of God.

Have you ever wondered why God changed Abram's and Sarai's names? God made this change at the same time He gave him instructions for circumcision, which marked Abraham and the promised multitudes to follow as partners in God's covenant. But why change their names too? It is believed the Hebrew people were the first people to use the letter *hei*. It marked their dedication to God. In the Ancient Near East, *elym* was a common word for god, any god.

Linguists suggest *hei* was inserted into the word to create the name *Elohim,* a Hebrew name to reference *the* God, belonging to the Hebrews: "Behold, this is our God."

When God established His chosen people though Abram and Sara, He required the sign of circumcision to mark them as His. Likewise, God breathed *hei* into their names. Abram became Abra**h**am and Sarai became Sara**h**. "Behold, these are my people."

When we choose to accept God's gift of salvation through Christ, He breathes into us His Spirit, *hei*, to mark and seal those who are His forever (Ephesians 1:13). Even if you find yourself traveling a desert in life and questioning God's presence, remember you are beheld as His. Like Abraham and Sarah, He will never leave you or forsake you (Hebrews 13:5).

Pause and Reflect

1. What would my name sound like with a *hei* inserted? I am a new creation in Christ. What is my new name?

   _____

   _____

   _____

2. God speaks best in the quiet whispers. How can I adjust my day to best hear the quiet words of His heart?

   _____

   _____

   _____

Praying the *Alef-Bet*

Lord, You sent Your Holy Spirit as a seal over me to mark me as Yours. Remind me of this truth as I face each day with the promise of Your presence and an understanding of how You see me. Amen.

VAV

She rises also while it is still night and gives food to her household
and portions to her maidens. —Proverbs 31:15

S tacey had finally agreed to meet her friend at church. She had to
admit, while waiting at the door scanning the parking lot, she was
a little excited. Stacey recalled her honest admission that church
was not a priority but agreed she needed to reconnect with Christ. *My
life is a little messy. It feels as though a darkness hovers over me and
distorts my view of God.*

Stacey spotted her friend walking toward her and waved. She lifted a
final prayer. *God, Your light reveals truth. If I am going to have a better
future, I need to nail down what I really believe about a relationship with
You.*

Vav—the Nail

Vav's word picture is a nail. It refers to binding and securing. In Hebrew,
vav is the conjunction *and*, which begins verse 15. It doesn't show up in
the English translation because we don't usually start sentences with a
conjunction. In Hebrew, the actions of verse 14 continue into verse 15.
The strong woman will be moved by the Holy Spirit, *and*, if necessary,
she will rise early while it is still dark.

The Hebrew word for night is *layil*. It means to twist or fold away.
As our day comes to an end, God folds up and tucks away the sunlight

and unfolds it again the next day. There are times in our lives when we may prefer darkness because it hides the difficult realities of our life. The Proverbs woman folds away the darkness and embraces the light of a new day with Christ.

Food in this verse is *terep,* but it can also be translated as "plunder," like the spoils of war. You see, the Proverbs woman is so firmly attached to Christ that her loved ones receive the plunder, the overflow, of her connection to Him. She portions the "meat" of her relationship with Christ because man cannot live on bread alone (Matthew 4:4).

Women are hard workers. We strive to complete all that needs to be done, but there are days we may feel as though we are blindly stumbling through the dark. When we bind ourselves to Christ, He dispels the darkness. He is the light of the world. When our connection with Him is secure, He helps us prioritize how we portion our time with Him, our family, and our responsibilities.

Proverbs 31 takes a turn in the next group of verses, but a foundation has been laid to ensure the strength of this woman as she prepares for battle.

Pause and Reflect

1. *Alef*—How have I placed God first?

2. *Bet*—How have I invited Christ to make His home in my heart?

3. *Gimel*—How do I depend on the support of the Holy Spirit?

_____

_____

_____

_____

_____

4. *Dalet*—How is my life set apart for Christ?

_____

_____

_____

_____

_____

5. *Hei*—How do I allow the Holy Spirit to direct me?

_____

_____

_____

_____

_____

6. *Vav*—How do I remain firmly attached to Christ?

_____

_____

_____

_____

_____

Praying the *Alef-Bet*

Lord, as I face my responsibilities in life, remind me that I am bound to Your heart. Your promises and precepts are secured with the connecting strength of *vav*. As I portion my time, help me nail down Your truth so I am not overwhelmed by the darkness of this world. Amen.

ZAYIN

She considers a field and buys it;
from her earnings she plants a vineyard. —Proverbs 31:16

Living on the mission field was difficult. Every victory was hard fought. Yet here Kellye was in an Eastern European country, far from home. She prayed for this for years, but the daily battles with the culture and loneliness were taking a toll. Was it a mistake moving here? Kellye felt dried and withered on the vine.

God, I know I didn't hear this call You placed on us wrong. I need to remember wherever I am, at home or on a mission filed, You plant us to grow spiritual fruit. I'm charged with cultivating this vineyard You have placed me in, and I need Your proper tools.

Zayin—the Weapon

Proverbs 31:16 introduces a new topic for the strong woman. Her investment into her home has gained fruit, and now she must consider or evaluate a new field in which to plant. The word considers, *zamam,* is the memory trigger beginning with *zayin*. It implies she first looks to identify what might prevent growth in her investment, and then she plans. Like a military warrior she does reconnaissance work, and there are times she must defend her investment.

The word picture for *zayin* is a sword. Swords are used as both weapons and tools. God's Word is described as His sword of the Spirit.

He provides it to us so we can defend ourselves against the dark forces of this world. When we plant ourselves and begin to bear fruit for God, Satan's response is to plant seeds of doubt, which can grow into wild vines and choke us out. We must then use our swords to prune and cut back his hindering vines of deceit and doubt so we can be healthy and productive. *Zayin*, His Word, is our sword.

Pause and Reflect

1. How regularly do I read Scripture to know it accurately?

_____

_____

_____

_____

2. How often do I ask the Holy Spirit to enlighten me to interpret and apply the Word faithfully so I can defend my faith? My calling? My family?

_____

_____

_____

_____

3. What choking vines do I need to clear so I can be more productive in God's vineyard?

_____

_____

_____

_____

Praying the *Alef-Bet*

Lord, You provide me with the power of Your Word as my sword of defense. I pray I handle it accurately with Your insight and guidance. Help me to consider and evaluate every place I have planted myself so I can faithfully produce Your fruit in my life. Amen.

EZER

Then the LORD God said, "It is not good for the man to be alone;
I will make him a helper suitable for him." —Genesis 2:18

G od called His masterpiece into existence, and it was good. Each firmly planted, lush green tree produced food pleasing to the eyes and taste buds. The four babbling rivers called Pishon, Gihon, Tigris, and Euphrates were bound within their shores. Each animal was fashioned from the ground. His highest creation was man, made in His image. He placed man into the garden with the command to cultivate and protect that which he came from. Nowhere was found another like man. And so God blessed man with the help of a strong woman.

Ezer—the Help of Strength

I'm curious. How would you define "helper suitable" in Genesis 2:18? Eve is described as Adam's helper, his assistant, and partner. I've even heard her labeled as Adam's "little helper." Excuse me while I unclench my teeth.

The Hebrew word is *ezer*. It does mean help, but it's help with warrior strength. Genesis 2:18 is the first time this word is used in the Bible, but the same word is used to describe the archangel Michael's actions in Daniel 10:13 and the men of valor in Joshua 1:14. It portrays the gift of strength God provided Adam. Adam was given the responsibility to

24

cultivate the garden. If we follow God's design plan, then Eve's duty was to nurture Adam. She, and all Proverb 31 Women, can best do this through prayer and submission to the leadings of the Holy Spirit as she honors her husband.

Consider this. When a king conquered a city, his forces preceded him as he marched in and took possession. The help of strength that went before him is *ezer*. Women are to be this for their husbands. They go before God's throne in intercession so their men can take their rightful positions and lead the family. This same thought can be applied to our relationship with Christ as well. As we interact, serve, and share the gospel of Jesus Christ with others we are preparing the way for Christ to take His place in our lives and theirs.

Pause and Reflect

1. How can I best be God's *ezer* to prepare a way through which others will encounter Him?

_____

_____

_____

_____

2. If married, how can I be my husband's *ezer*? If not married, to whom is God calling me to be like an *ezer*?

_____

_____

_____

_____

_____

3. How easily do I accept that God bestows me with great strength to be used in prayer, intercession, and discernment?

_____

_____

_____

_____

Praying the *Alef-Bet*

Lord, You are my great help in times of trouble. Teach me to be the same for others through Your strength. Lord, thank You for my position as *ezer*. May I go before others in Your might as You take Your rightful place in our lives and we submit to Your lead. Amen.

CHET

She girds herself with strength and makes her arms strong.
—Proverbs 31:17

Terri exhaled and hung her head. Was she defeated? Was all hope lost?

Lord, I pray for my children every day. I pray they find favor with their peers. I pray for their abilities and safety. I thought we had a firm foundation in You! Tears fell gently from her face as she wiped her nose and gulped a breath. This was not what she expected. One of her children wandered outside of the boundaries she faithfully established. Were her prayers wasted?

Oh, Father, why? Please don't be silent.

His peace slowly eased over Terri as she heard Him speak to her heart. *Beloved, your foundation is firm, but your walls are not high enough. Gird yourself with My strength. I will make your arms strong. Now, like Nehemiah, you must rebuild your walls.*

Chet—the Fence or Wall

When stable and high, walls define boundaries, protect what is inside, and keep danger out. When shaky and crumbling, they require reinforcement. Proverbs 31:17 begins with the letter *chet*, in the Hebrew word gird, and it holds the word picture of a fence or wall.

Proverbs shares that the strong woman will gird, put on, strength. *Oz* is the word for strength. It is a root for the word *ezer*. She puts on her God-given strength and picks up *zayin*, her sword. She has work to do and a wall to reinforce. She knows her power comes from prayer and her yoke to Christ.

You may have prayed that God would surround your loved ones with a hedge of protection. This is *chet*. A strong woman recognizes a wall must be built, inspected, and reinforced if it is to be effective because danger lurks in many forms. We will face hard times, but we are strengthened when we place ourselves behind God's protection and boundaries.

Pause and Reflect

1. What in my life needs strength from God? What do I need to gird myself with—patience, endurance, faith?

   _____

   _____

   _____

2. When was the last time I inspected my wall? How shall I ask the Lord to reveal ways the enemy might seek to breach my wall of protection?

   _____

   _____

   _____

Praying the *Alef-Bet*

Lord, Your Word tells me You are my fortress where I can take refuge (Psalm 18:2). I pray You will surround my loved ones with Your protection both physically and spiritually. Reveal to me any areas in our wall requiring Your reinforcement. Gird me with Your strength to fight the good fight as I stand behind You in prayer for those I love. Amen.

CHUPPAH

For this reason, a man shall leave his father and his mother,
and be joined to his wife; and they shall become one flesh.
—Genesis 2:24

The sun was setting, but there was no hurry to leave. He treasured his time of prayer. As Isaac lifted his eyes, he noticed a caravan approaching. He followed the steady pace of the camel's black silhouette against the jewel-colored sky.

Rebekah studied his face as she approached from a distance. Her camel stopped and kneeled for her dismount. She turned to ask the servant holding her beast, "Who is that man walking to meet us?"

Shielding his eyes against the setting sun, the servant answered, "He is Isaac, my master, your betrothed."

Isaac entered the area with confidence as Rebekah moved to cover herself with the veil. She stood quietly as the servant relayed the events of the past several weeks. Taking her by the hand, Isaac brought her into his mother Sarah's tent. Rebekah became his wife, and he loved her (Genesis 24:62–67).

Chuppah—the Marriage Canopy

Weddings have sure changed since I was married. The simple ceremony and church hall reception has been replaced with barns, glamourous venues, and destinations. I know—two of my three children have married, and the details were never-ending. One item I wish they had incorporated into the ceremony was the Jewish *chuppah.*

The *chuppah,* which begins with the letter chet, is the canopy used in Jewish wedding ceremonies. The covering represents the spirit of God hovering over marriage, establishing a new household, and girding it with His strength. The two will enter as individuals but leave as one with God's Spirit and begin to build their home.

When building a brand-new home, we can select never-used materials to create a home free of flaws. But what happens when a couple moves into a dilapidated fixer-upper riddled with problems? It will take significant work to do repairs and renovations, but it will never be free of flaws. Our marriages, homes, and families will never wholly resemble perfection because we are all fixer-uppers. We may feel as though our arms must be strong to carry such weight, but our restoration is only possible through the grace of God and His presence hovering over us. He desires to take us by the hand, love us, and lead us to the protection of His chuppah, His covering.

Pause and Reflect

1. What areas in my life require God's restoration? Am I willing to allow Him to rebuild?

_____

_____

_____

_____

_____

_____

_____

_____

2. Jews believe the contents of a home are not important; rather, it is the people and the hospitality they extend that makes a home. What is one way I can extend hospitality to others and help them experience God's spirit hovering over my home?

_____

_____

_____

_____

_____

_____

_____

_____

Praying the *Alef-Bet*

Lord, You are ever-present. Even now Your Spirit hovers over my home and family. Thank You that in You, although we are not perfect, we can experience a renovation of our hearts. Thank You for loving me well. Amen.

TET

She senses that her gain is good;
her lamp does not go out at night. —Proverbs 31:18

They finally made it out of the house with only a few minor meltdowns. One couldn't find his shoes, and the other didn't want to drink out of the yellow sippy cup. Why are Sunday mornings so challenging? Elizabeth strapped her troop into their car seats. As her husband sat with the car idling, she ran back in to find her Bible.

After a few minutes of glancing around the room, she gave up and headed back to the car before another meltdown ensued. Climbing into the car, she saw her Bible sitting on the floorboard. A sigh escaped her as she realized it was right where she left it last week.

Elizabeth's mind wandered as she looked out the window. *I faithfully bring my kids to church every Sunday. We even say our bedtime prayers. I know I'm doing what I should, and it's good, right? God is good, and I believe in Him, but is there more? The pastor talks about producing fruit. Am I doing that?*

Tet—the Snake

Proverbs 31:16–18 describes how the strong woman defends her faith and family like a warrior.

- *Zayin*—She wields God's Word like a sword.
- *Chet*—She prayerfully builds a wall of protection.
- *Tet*—She tests her actions to ensure they align with God's will.

The letter *tet*, and its word picture of a snake, begins the verse in the word *tamah*, which means to sense or perceive. Consider how a snake evaluates its surroundings. It must get close enough to flick its tongue in order to taste and sense where it is. *Tet* is a letter of contrast. It is a root letter in the Hebrew words for good, safe, seduce, and slaughter. Do you see the contrast?

Here in Proverbs, the strong woman must evaluate the contrasts her life presents—holy versus evil and right versus wrong. The verse also holds a bit of wordplay. The Hebrew word for night means a twisting away of the light, like a writhing snake. When I think of snakes in the Bible, my mind immediately goes to the serpent in the garden. This time, through God's yoke of strength and the leading of the Holy Spirit, we do not need to fall to Satan's lies and twist away from the light. When faced with actions, attitudes, adversity, and opportunities, we can give them all a taste test to determine if they contrast with God's plan for our life. Taste and see that the Lord is good (Psalm 34:8).

Pause and Reflect

1. What areas in my life require God's taste test?

_____

_____

_____

_____

_____

2. How can I deepen my relationship with Christ so I can sense Him more and better evaluate the world's contrasts?

_____

_____

_____

_____

_____

_____

_____

3. Are you settling for the good in life, or do you seek God's very best? How can you sense the difference?

_____

_____

_____

_____

_____

_____

_____

Praying the *Alef-Bet*

Lord, I seek to honor You in every way. I desire to relish Your goodness. Help me taste test all I encounter and do for You so the fruit I produce is a great gain for Your kingdom. Lord, give me the strength to resist the serpent's lies so I can honor You. Amen.

ל

YUD

She stretches out her hands to the distaff, and her hands
grasp the spindle. —Proverbs 31:19

A smile spread across Lisa's face as the couple left her office. Like her, they were first-time homeowners in their family. And like her, their journey began with many strikes against them. Poverty, abuse, and being a high school drop-out were just some of the stigmas Lisa fought to overcome as she worked to achieve her position in life. The long-ago memories bubbled up from her past. With a confirming peace, she honored the memory of someone helping her just as she helped that couple.

I have the authority to serve and love others because Christ did the same for me through people I encountered. He lives and loves through my hands reaching out to others. What an honor it is to weave into the lives of others.

Yud—the Hand

Yud is the smallest Hebrew letter, not much bigger than an apostrophe. *Yud's* word picture is a hand, and it represents power, authority, and ownership. Verse 19 marks a new topic for the strong woman, her hands of authority and service. The verse indicates she works with yarns and textiles and stretches her hand toward the spindle. When the Bible references an outstretched hand, it usually relates to military action, like when God demonstrated His power through Moses's outstretched hand against Egypt (Exodus 4—10). It also refers to authority, like when King Ahasuerus extended his hand, holding a scepter to Esther (Esther 5:2).

The Proverbs woman's hands work with the same influence. Whether you work with textiles or not, when you extend your hand to others, you are weaving into their lives. When God leads your hand—one of the smallest parts of your body—it holds power as it acts on behalf of Jesus Christ.

Pause and Reflect

1. What authority has God granted me to weave into the lives of others?

_____

_____

_____

_____

2. How has God displayed His power through me?

_____

_____

_____

_____

Praying the *Alef-Bet*

Lord, I pray I will not miss opportunities to extend my hand to others. I have much to offer, and I can do all things through Your strength and authority. Thank You, Lord, for all who have extended their hands to me. Amen.

KAF

She extends her hand to the poor, and she stretches out
her hands to the needy. —Proverbs 31:20

Kathi embraced her friend. "How can I pray for you today?"

"I don't know. I'm just not cut out for this job. I don't have the finesse others seem to have. They do this position so much better than me." Kathi's friend shook her head in defeat.

Lord, help me say what my friend needs to hear. Kathi lifted a silent prayer as she listened to her friend, then spoke. "It sounds like you have a raging case of 'poor me.' If God put you in this position, you are held in His hand. He is holding and molding you."

"But what can I do?"

She extended her hand to her friend. "You can let me pray with you. Let's ask Him to tuck you under His wing and provide your needs."

Kaf—the Cupped Hand, the Wing

Kaf is the second Hebrew letter with the word picture of a hand. Unlike *yud*, which is an image of a hand grasping power, this hand is an open, cupped palm. The idea is that our hand molds and shapes that which it holds. The cupped hand also relates to the idea of a wing. (I'm now imagining you flapping your cupped hands.)

In Proverbs 31:20, the strong woman recognizes the needs of others. The context suggests a physical or financial need, but the word poor is the same word used to describe those who are poor in spirit and those who need to know Jesus. I know the desperation of that need. God placed women in my life who extended their hands of friendship. Some were mentors or prayer partners who held me accountable. Each helped shape and mold my faith. They taught me to tuck myself under God's protective wing and submit to His leadership in response to my love for Him.

Pause and Reflect

1. How has God lovingly held me in His cupped hand? How is He molding me?

   _____

   _____

   _____

   _____

2. How can I extend my open hand to those around me who are poor in spirit?

   _____

   _____

   _____

   _____

Praying the *Alef-Bet*

Lord, You extend Your hand of strength to me, but that same hand holds and protects me. Send others into my life who will extend godly advice, pray with me, and provide the blessing of friendship as my needs arise. And may I be the same for others. Amen.

KOHEN

But you are a chosen race, a royal priesthood, a holy nation,
a people for God's own possession, so that you may proclaim
the excellencies of Him who has called you out of darkness
into His marvelous light. —1 Peter 2:9

KEN

For as many as are the promises of God, in Him they are yes.
—2 Corinthians 1:20

When I read Exodus 19, I imagine the Israelites settling themselves before Mount Sinai after wondering the desert for months. The elders assemble quickly as Moses prepares to speak the word he received from the Lord. They dared not waste time. As Moses sits before them, a hush falls.

"House of Jacob, you witnessed what I did to Egypt, and how I bore you on eagles' wings and brought you to myself. Now, if you indeed obey My voice and keep My covenant, then you shall be My own possession, and you shall be to Me a kingdom of priests and a holy nation."

I can almost hear murmurs of agreement as they ripple through the group. This is their heart's desire. They will follow the Lord. The people answer together and say, "Yes, all that the Lord has spoken we will do!"

Moses stands and slowly begins the climb back up the mount. He brings back the word of the people to the Lord. "Yes."

Kohen (Priest), *Ken* (Yes)—The Yes of God's Priest

Proverbs 31 not only contains military references, but it also points to the Tabernacle, the priests, and their clothing. The roles of the priests were vast in ancient Israel and included maintaining the Tabernacle, blessings, offerings, and sacrifices. As God's chosen, the priests opened their hand and said yes to the activity of God's service. The word yes in ancient Hebrew is spelled *kaf, nun.* The word pictures represent an open hand to life. Like the ancient priest, the Proverbs woman is someone who assists in molding us into the likeness of God.

Today, the glory of the Lord no longer dwells in the Tabernacle but in the hearts of believers who have surrendered their will to the Lord. Jesus extended His hand to us, the poor in spirit. When we recognize our poverty, God holds us in His cupped hand and molds us into His image. We minister as the ancient priests did by saying yes to the activities of God's service and leading others to their opportunity to say yes to the Lord.

Pause and Reflect

1. Is my hand open to receive the life God has for me, or is it closed?

_____

_____

_____

_____

_____

2. If God considers me His priest, how am I revealing His heart to others?

_____

_____

_____

_____

_____

Praying the *Alef-Bet*

Lord, I pray with hands held high and palms open to receive Your yes over my life. I realize, like You desired for the children of Israel, You desire my very best. I am to act as Your priest in this world and reveal Your heart to others so they too can experience Your yes in their lives. Help me proclaim Your excellencies. Amen.

ל

LAMED

She is *not* afraid of the snow for her household,
for all her household are clothed with scarlet.
—Proverbs 31:21 (emphasis added)

W e're going to have to let you go." How many times did Marie's mind repeat that dreadful statement during her commute home? What would now be her last commute from a job she worked at for six years.

What am I going to do? She sighed. *I need to talk to mama.* The shock swelled to anger, which dissolved into worry as she anticipated a long, cold season of unemployment. Marie quickly decided to detour from the route and head to her mama's house.

Walking into the house, Marie smiled as her mom greeted her from that old, overstuffed brown chair where she faithfully read her Bible every evening. The floor lamp was tilted just right over the page. Mama looked up. "Well, hey, honey, you stopped by."

It all came tumbling out. "I've lost my job. They downsized my department and let me go. I'm worried, Mama. What if it takes forever to find something else? What if my savings run out? What if . . ."

Mama laid her open Bible on her lap and reached for her daughter's hand. "What if you worrying doesn't add another day? What if we look at what the Bible says about all this worry? You know, God's Word is always our best teacher when we have so many questions."

Mama always responded this way. She lovingly prodded others to look at God's Word first when they had a lesson to learn.

Lamed—the Teaching Goad

Lamed stands in the center of the Hebrew alphabet as the tallest letter. It resembles a walking stick, and the word picture is a goad, which was used to prod and direct oxen. Therefore the letter relates to learning and training.

The strong woman of Proverbs does not fear winter; her family is clothed with scarlet. This verse parallels the metaphorical bleak winters of life, the hard times we will inevitably face. When we too know we are covered in scarlet—the scarlet blood of Christ—we do not need to fear our winters in life. Where better to learn this, and so many more of God's promises, than in His Word? Salvation is the greatest lesson of God's good news, but the Bible also teaches us about worry, relationships, finances, and so much more. As we read, the Holy Spirit prods, leads, and directs us toward God's truth.

Pause and Reflect

1. What biblical topic would I like to learn more about?

_____

_____

_____

_____

_____

_____

_____

2. How often do I turn to God's Word to lead and teach me? Can I challenge myself to find and meditate on two verses about my topic? Was my understanding redirected, or was I prodded to continue?

_____

_____

_____

_____

_____

_____

_____

Praying the *Alef-Bet*

Lord, Thank You for Your Word. It reveals Your heart and precepts on all I face each day. I pray it teaches, leads, and directs me in understanding Your will and when making decisions. I pray I do not kick against Your training but submit graciously to Your lead. Amen.

MEM

She makes coverings for herself;
her clothing is fine linen and purple. —Proverbs 31:22

The emotions crashed over her yet again. The words *worthless*, *shame*, and *oblivious* raged in the chaos of her mind. Her depression ebbed and flowed, but today she felt her anxiety swelling and threatening to burst forth from her dam of resolve.

"This is so hard and exhausting." She ran through the mantra that usually calmed the storm. *Nothing is due. I haven't missed a deadline. No one is expecting me.*

Breathe in; breathe out.

The side effects of her depression were a slippery slope. Her medication and counseling helped, but it also helped to cover herself in prayer and be reminded of how God viewed her: clothed in fine splendor.

Mem—Water, Life, Chaos

Mem's word picture is water and carries the ideas of chaos, like water thundering downstream. *Mem* begins Proverbs 31:22 in the Hebrew word for coverlet, the bedspread the woman in Proverbs is making to cover herself. I often want to bury myself deep under the covers when the chaos of my mind begins to stir. Can you relate? We may not be weavers or seamstresses, but we can be tempted to cover ourselves with shame, grief, or pain instead of the dignified clothing of the King's daughter.

Jesus offers us something different. Think of making a bed. We shake out and smooth the covers over the bed. Water moves in a similar way. When released, it flows out and covers the land. This is how Jesus offers His grace. He washes us clean as He spreads His life-giving, living waters over us. When we accept this gift, we can put on His clothing of linen and purple, which was the fabric and color used in the Tabernacle—His dwelling place.

Pause and Reflect

1. What areas in my life require God's cleansing?

_____

_____

_____

_____

2. What can I spread out before God and release so I can be cleansed and accept His priestly garments of linen and purple?

_____

_____

_____

_____

Praying the *Alef-Bet*

Lord, with a word, You stilled the storm and calmed the sea. There are days I feel as though waves are thundering through my mind. I pray Your Word will calm the chaos I face in all situations. Thank You that I do not need to hide from Your presence, but instead, I am clothed in the fine, purple linen that reflects Your dwelling place in my heart. Thank You, Jesus. Amen.

מִקְוֶה

MIKVEH

If we confess our sins, He is faithful and righteous to forgive us
our sins and to cleanse us from all unrighteousness. —1 John 1:9

T he priest opened the massive curtains and entered the Tabernacle's outer court. He was tasked with changing the shewbread, and he would stand in God's presence, which dwelled with them in the holy of holies. This thought humbled him, and he stumbled slightly under the weight of his fear and reverence for *Elohim*, God Almighty. He surveyed the courtyard. Placed in front of the holy place was the massive bronze laver. Yes, he must wash his hands and feet just as the Lord required. But standing before the laver was the altar of sacrifice, and he began his service there. Just as the Lord commanded—a sacrifice must be made and blood must be shed before cleansing is to take place (Exodus 40:32).

Mikveh—the Ceremonial Bath and Cleansing

Although the Hebrew word *mikveh* is not mentioned in the Proverbs 31 passage, it does begin with the letter *mem* and relates to water. Have you ever wondered where the practice of baptism originated? It is rooted in the process of the *mikveh*, which is a bath Jews use for ritual cleansing and purification. The Hebrew word for hope is contained within the letters spelling *mikveh*. Hope is spelled, *kaph, vav, hei*. Baptism symbolizes our hope when we commit our lives to Christ, and death gives way to life. As strong women, our hope in Christ is the wellspring of our faith.

To be clean means we are free from contamination, but we are never pure before God without the covering and cleansing of Christ's bloodshed. God used the Tabernacle to point to His plan of redemption. A sacrifice must take place before cleansing and entering His presence. Baptism follows the acknowledgment of Christ's sacrifice.

Pause and Reflect

1. Can I stand with confidence in the presence of the Lord, or does the contamination of sin linger?

   _____

   _____

   _____

   _____

2. Jesus' sacrifice was once and final. Do I acknowledge His sacrifice? How do I confess my sin and accept the cleansing power of His living water?

   _____

   _____

   _____

   _____

Praying the *Alef-Bet*

Lord, thank You for Your sacrifice. It removes the contamination of sin and, like the *mikveh*, cleanses me. Father, thank You that I can stand in Your presence with confidence in Your sacrifice and purification. It is an honor to wear the clean, white robes of Your righteousness. Amen.

NUN

Her husband is known in the gates,
when he sits among the elders of the land. —Proverbs 31:23

I'm so proud of the job my husband is doing," her friend commented. Lauren smiled. She really was pleased for her friend, but as a single woman, Lauren wondered when she would experience the joy of celebrating a husband. As she left lunch and returned to her car, Lauren confessed the doubt and sadness that seemed to chase her down when confronted with her continued single status. The click of the seatbelt was a reminder of God's continuous hold on her. Lauren recalled the promise in Isaiah 62:5—just as the bridegroom rejoices over the bride, your God rejoices over you. *Yes, Lord, and I am proud to honor Your faithfulness in my life. You are my Bridegroom. I am pleased to make You known.*

Nun—the Fish and Life

Proverbs 31:23 is considered the main idea of the acrostic poem. All that the Proverbs woman of biblical times did brought honor to her husband who sat at the city gates. In turn, he acknowledged and praised her, which is the second half of the poem.

The city gate was the hub of life in ancient cities. The market was there, and it was at the gate where the judges and elders dispensed their wisdom. Verse 23 and *nun* represent the life of the city. *Nun's* word picture is a fish. When we think of the lively action of a swimming fish or how it wiggles on a hook, we can imagine how *nun* relates to life and activity. To be seated and known at the ancient city gate was a great honor. A wife would be proud to have such a husband.

How does this verse apply today? What is the widow to do? Or a divorced woman or a woman never married? How can this poem relate to her? After the betrothal ceremony, a Jewish bridegroom returns to his father's house to prepare for his bride to join him. This is what Jesus describes when He mentions in the Book of John that He is returning to His father's house to prepare a place for us (John 14:3). Jesus is our Bridegroom. He calls us His beloved. What a joy it is to make His name known at the city gates, our place of action and life. Strong woman, all you do supports and honors His name and proclaims His redemption.

Pause and Reflect

1. How can knowing God describes me as His beloved help while I await my Bridegroom's return?

_____

_____

_____

2. How does my daily life honor my Bridegroom, Jesus Christ?

_____

_____

_____

Praying the *Alef-Bet*

Lord, it is my desire to make Your name famous at the city gates and throughout this land. It is an honor to be Your bride, and I pray that all I do brings honor to You. Amen.

SAMECH

She makes linen garments and sells them,
and supplies belts to the tradesmen. —Proverbs 31:24

C hris caught herself falling back into that dark place where doubts grow and questions rear with ugly heads. *Why did you make that promise? You're not the same person you were all those years ago. If he truly loved you, he would consider your happiness.*

"No." She rebuked those thoughts. *I promised my husband I would honor his desire not to have children—for better and for worse. Just because I have doubts years later doesn't mean I can renege on my promise. It was made with full knowledge of what I was getting into.* Chris consciously shifted her mind to a place of resolve. *My promise is like a tent rope, attached to a peg and driven into the ground. If I dig it up now, our secure line of trust and support will become loose. No, that peg of support needs to remain reliable.*

Samech—the Support, the Peg

Proverbs 31:24 begins with the fifteenth letter of the Hebrew alphabet, *samech*, which is often linked to marriage. Its word picture is a peg, used to support a tent. Combined with the notion that some think the letter resembles a ring, with no beginning and no end, we can begin to understand *samech's* link to marriage.

The Proverbs woman supports her family by selling items in the marketplace. But remember, linen can point to priestly garments, and the previous verse referenced her bridegroom. It is also helpful to know the word tradesmen, to whom she is selling her merchandise, is a representation of the Canaanites, Israel's enemies. In her day-to-day life, the Proverbs woman interacted with her enemy. To prevent their enticement, she remained securely attached to her faith and continued to weave linen, a reminder of her priestly commitment to God and the honor she brings Him.

In biblical times, couples didn't see each during their betrothal but prepared independently for their wedding and life together. The bride made herself ready by making her wedding dress. In a similar way, believers in Jesus are living in the betrothal period between Jesus and His bride, the church. We must prepare ourselves while waiting for our Bridegroom and make His name known. Our preparations include our righteous acts, which will become the clean, white linen of our wedding attire (Revelation 19:8).

When we make a commitment to follow Christ, we are also committing to support His bride, the church. Like in marriage, the goal of the church is to support each other and honor the yoke, but when individuals have separate goals, this becomes a challenge. For some, the church is a place of comfort and solace. Others have been burned by the church and still feel the sting. The Bible suggests the church supports each other through love (John 13:34), not judging one another (Romans 14:13), and by pursuing peace, kindness, and forgiveness (Romans 14:19 and Ephesians 4:32). Our commitment to Christ is a marriage covenant. *Samech* reminds us of His never-ending support.

Pause and Reflect

1. As a bride of Christ my wedding attire is considered my righteous acts (Revelation 19:8). How well am I weaving my wedding attire? Are there areas I can better support other followers of Christ?

_____

_____

_____

_____

2. What support do I need from the Holy Spirit to help me better wait for my Bridegroom's return?

_____

_____

_____

_____

Praying the *Alef-Bet*

Lord, waiting is often difficult. While I await Your return and the time You will be reunited with Your bride, the church, I pray that I am working to prepare and support her. I pray I can show her love, kindness, and forgiveness. Thank You for the support You offer me through the Holy Spirit and Your body of believers. Amen.

AYIN

Strength and dignity are her clothing,
and she smiles at the future. —Proverbs 31:25

Stephanie could barely contain the joy she felt; she was almost giddy. Did she just skip? She couldn't help but chuckle. Her blossoming relationship with Christ had lifted such a weight from her. Years of pain and bad decisions in her life seemed to be melting away. She was truly becoming a new creation. *Oh, I wish my husband could experience this freedom as well.*

A quiet, confirming peace responded. "Daughter, lift up your eyes and look to the field. The harvest is ready."

The newness of Stephanie's relationship with the God of the universe made her pause. She didn't want to miss a thing. *Lord, are You giving me a glimpse of my husband's salvation?* Her smile beamed; his future held as much hope as hers. *I know it may take time, and I pray You will strengthen me during the wait. I know You have Your eyes on him too.*

Ayin—the Eye, the Source

Proverbs 31:25 begins with the Hebrew letter *ayin*, which holds the word picture of and is the Hebrew word for eye. Eyes have long represented both sight and understanding. You might recall the common idiom we use such as "I see" meaning, "I understand."

Does looking toward the future give you joy or stress? Does it leave you with questions? The strong woman can hold her head high with dignity and look to the future with a heart of laughter. I would love a dose of her confidence. Proverbs 31 offers a blueprint for this joy. It builds as we yoke ourselves to Christ and live a purposeful life set apart for Him. It strengthens as we do battle on the front lines for our loved ones. It overflows as we extend our hand in service, and it can be unstoppable as we learn the depths of His cleansing power and the support He offers us. When I look back at the verses of Proverbs and see the foundation laid, I can look forward and smile.

Pause and Reflect

1. How do I celebrate when I look at my past and recognize the changes God has made in my life?

_____

_____

_____

2. How does knowing God's eyes remain on me with a keen understanding of what I need help me look toward the future with a smile?

_____

_____

_____

Praying the *Alef-Bet*

Lord, Your eye is on me. Knowing this truth reaffirms in my spirit that You perceive my every need and struggle. Father, help me to recall and count my many blessings so I can look to the future with smiling confidence of Your continued presence. Amen.

פ

PEH

She opens her mouth in wisdom, and the teaching
of kindness is on her tongue. —Proverbs 31:26

How are you not devastated or angry? How can you possibly offer me words of encouragement? You are facing the most difficult period of a life filled with repeated pounding waves of despair, and you're telling me to hang in there?" Cynthia's friend shook her head and gave Cynthia her full attention. "I'm serious. How can you speak with such wisdom and kindness?"

Cynthia paused for a moment and considered the question. Her wisdom came from experience, but her kindness only came from embracing the loving-kindness of Christ. She pressed into Him daily. To be honest, there were moments Cynthia needed to get face to face with Him and feel the breath of His mouth over her just to survive.

She answered her friend's question. "I can only speak of what I've walked through. He promises to never leave me or forsake me, and I have tasted the kindness of the Lord. Things are not perfect in my life, but I serve a perfect God, and He stands with me."

Peh—the Mouth

Proverbs 31:26 describes the strong woman speaking with wisdom and kindness. Reading this verse helps us relate *peh's* word picture, the mouth, to the verse. The Bible refers to the mouth more than four hundred times and has another 10,330 references to speech. The mouth holds great power to create or destroy.

Peh is also the first letter of the Hebrew word for face, *penay*. There's a meme floating around social media that says, "Controlling my tongue is no problem. It's my face that needs deliverance." Can you relate?

I'm quick to offer my opinion, but to truly offer God's wisdom, I need to spend time with Him face to face. I'm willing to admit I often face times when speaking with kindness is difficult. When I pause to remember the kindness God grants me, I am able to readjust my attitude. There is a saying that kindness is the language the deaf can hear and the blind can see. I want to be known for my wisdom and kindness.

Pause and Reflect

1. What wisdom of God would I consider as the most important to speak?

_____

_____

_____

2. How would I describe the words I speak? Wise? Loving? Kind? Firm? Sharp? Weak?

_____

_____

_____

Praying the *Alef-Bet*

Lord, my mouth holds power, and I pray that power is under Your control. I desire to be known as a woman of wisdom and kindness. Please put words into my mouth that best reflect Your influence in my heart. Amen.

TZADI

She looks well to the ways of her household.
—Proverbs 31:27

While putting the laundry away, Tara found drug paraphernalia in her son's drawer. Shock reverberated through her system. Where did he find the drugs? She choked as the question caught in her throat. *I took every precaution. God, we raised our kids in a Christian home; how could this happen?* She sat down hard on her son's bed.

I was a stay-at-home mom, dedicated to raising my kids in a godly home. Now this? Tara exhaled as her head sank into her hands. Blame pushed out fear and settled itself firmly in her heart. *How could I miss this? Was I not paying attention? Have I failed as a mom?* Questions grew in her hurting heart. She knew God would respond in His time, so Tara wouldn't allow her faith to grow idle.

Tzadi—the Fishhook, the Righteous Man

Tzadi has two forms, straight and bent. Its pictograph is a fishhook, and it suggests an inescapable pull toward something. Some suggest the two forms represent how we can approach God: hooked and kneeling in surrender or standing captivated in His righteousness.

Proverbs 31:27 starts with the Hebrew word *tsaphah,* which means to lean forward and keep watch. On a few occasions the NASB translates the word as watchman, which reflects the military theme of the passage. Like a watchman on the wall, the strong woman leans in and keeps watch to warn her loved ones so they will not be lured away. Unfortunately, there are times when the enemy is able to set his hook, and a desperate tug of war ensures. When this happens, the strong woman will not sit idle and allow fear, doubt, or blame defeat her. She has too much to lose. In these times, it helps to pull out Proverbs 31 and review some of the imagery from the Hebrew alphabet, God's blueprint of strength.

- *Alef*—We are yoked to Him and have access to His strength.
- *Zayin*—He provides us with His sword of the Spirit.
- *Chet*—We can stand, firmly surrounded by His wall of refuge.
- *Yud*—We hold authority over the rulers, powers, the forces of darkness, and wickedness in the heavenly places.
- *Samech*—He supports us.
- *Ayin*—He gives us insight, and we are clothed in strength.
- *Peh*—We speak with wisdom.

This is the table from which we feast. Our faith will not grow idle, and the Bread of Life will sustain us.

Pause and Reflect

1. How comfortable am I warning others when I recognize sin dangling from a hook ready to snare them?

_____

_____

_____

_____

_____

_____

2. When I, or a loved one, am hooked by sin, how do I respond? Do I
   tend to become idle, or do you sound a battle cry?

_____

_____

_____

_____

_____

_____

Praying the *Alef-Bet*

Lord, help me lean in and watch carefully over those I love. When I
recognize the tempting hook of the enemy, remind me to gird myself
with Your strength and avoid idle faith. Amen.

LECHEM

She . . . does not eat the bread of idleness.
—Proverbs 31:27

Tara sat back satisfied. The same satisfaction she felt after enjoying a good meal. She had spent the last several months feasting on God's Word and storing His promises in her heart. And now she was seeing the results. Moments that once caused her to respond in anger, Tara could now, with God's strength, respond to them in peace. She easily recalled Bible verses that slashed through provoking words and fed her spirit joy. Tara no longer lived on table scraps but the bounty of God's table and His victorious life.

Lechem—Bread

Lechem means bread, but the root for this word is *chem*, which means anger and to fight. Think about how we knead bread by punching down the dough, and you can see the connection. And I wonder how many wars and disagreements through history were the result of anger over fields and food.

Matthew 4:4 tells us we will not live on bread alone but on every word from the mouth of God. I don't think it is a far stretch to consider the Word of God as the food, the bread, we are to survive on when we are angry or facing a battle. As we consume His Word, He consumes our hearts and our emotions and fights for us.

I wonder if there is a wordplay contained in Proverbs 31:27. The strong woman does not want her loved ones hooked and pulled away, so she keeps an eye on them. But if they *are* hooked, she will not sit and stew, allowing her anger to eat away at her, nor will she remain idle. Idle hands are the devil's tools. Instead, she will feast on God's Word and continue to speak with the wisdom and kindness she is known for. Part of praying for her daily bread includes asking God for her emotional and spiritual needs as well.

Pause and Reflect

1. Which Bible verses gives me the most comfort when I face hard times?

   _____

   _____

   _____

   _____

2. Does anger hold me captive? Or stress? Has my faith become idle? How often do I ask God to provide for my emotional and spiritual needs?

   _____

   _____

   _____

   _____

Praying the *Alef-Bet*

Lord, You are the only Bread of Life guaranteed to fully satisfy. I pray that Your Word will sustain me when I feel weak or am provoked, that I do not mishandle Your Word. Give to me Your daily bread. Amen.

QOF

Her children rise up and bless her; her husband also,
and he praises her. —Proverbs 31:28

J ulie smiled as he spoke but couldn't meet his eyes. He was asking
if she would allow their relationship to be exclusive. Was her heart
ready? To be honest, she loved him. Julie glanced back at him. He
was such a nice guy, but he needed a full understanding of what he was
getting into. A warning flashed through her mind. *When he knows, he
will run. No man wants to sign on with this hot mess.*

Still . . .

She formed her answer. "My past holds some serious sin. I am no
Proverbs 31 Woman."

"That's what you're afraid of?" He tilted his head. "I want to show
you something." He reached and pulled his wallet from his pocket.
He removed a folded piece of paper, and as he smoothed it across the
table, her heart skipped a beat. It was a page torn from a Bible, the
Proverbs 31 passage.

"As we've been dating these last few months, I've noticed how
you handle yourself, and how you speak to others. I've admired your
commitment to Christ." He paused. She was sure this was where he
would dismiss her.

"Almost daily, I recognized a characteristic in you that resembled the
woman in Proverbs 31, and I highlighted the verses you matched." Her
eyes went straight to the page he held in his hand and noticed nearly
every line was highlighted.

He continued, "There is a verse that speaks to the husband honoring this woman. You are deserving of this type of honor."

Qof—the Nape of the Neck, the Back of the Head

Proverbs 31:28 begins with the letter *qof*, which generally means the back of the head or what follows. Some think the written form looks like the arching dome of a head. This imagery links the letter to the idea of cycles.

We may face times when, no matter what, it seems sin or its consequences are right behind us, following in hot pursuit. The Proverbs woman acknowledges this, but she chooses to follow God's precepts. She lives God's holy cycle of obedience and girding His strength, which leads to service and satisfaction. Like the citizens of Zion mentioned in Isaiah 30:20–21, she may eat from the bread of adversity, but she hears the voice of the Lord behind her saying, "This is the way, walk in it." Others recognize the voice of the Lord in her and offer her well-deserved honor.

Pause and Reflect

1. What cycles do I recognize in my life? Am I trapped in a cycle of sin, or do I enjoy the freedom God's cycle of obedience provides?

_____

_____

_____

_____

_____

2. How comfortable am I receiving praise from others? How do I perceive and receive the praise God bestows over me?

_____

_____

_____

_____

_____

Praying the *Alef-Bet*

Lord, help me recognize the cycles in my life, both sin and victory. Help me walk in Your cycle of holiness and listen for Your voice behind me as You walk with me. Reveal Yourself and cleanse me as You lavish me with Your love and abundant favor. Amen.

אָשַׁר

ASHAR

Her children rise up and bless her; her husband also,
and he praises her. —Proverbs 31:28

I t was a few minutes before sunset on Friday. As the hostess approached the table, the guests settled around it quieted and stood. They watched as she struck the match and lit the four candles at the head of the table. Each represented the members of her family. As she finished, she allowed the match to fall to the tray to burn itself out. She motioned her hands over the flame three times as though she were drawing in and welcoming the presence of God. She dedicated their time with the opening blessing then covered her face and offered her personal silent prayer.

With the candle lighting complete, her guest opened their Shabbat dinner with a song of shalom, of peace. The next song, "Eishet Chayil," "Woman of Strength," was dedicated to the women at the table. It is a song celebrating their service to the family. It is a song celebrating their strength. They stood and blessed the women.

Ashar—Blessed

In Proverbs 31:28–29, the strong woman's children and husband are blessing her. Blessed is the word *ashar,* which contains the idea of setting straight and making progress, but it is also translated as "happy." If things are going well, and we are making progress, we tend to be happy. The imagery of the combined letters in *ashar* relates to the idea of fire on the head and symbolizes the presence of God. The Jewish Shabbat service on Friday night begins with the lighting of candles and welcoming the presence of God. It sets the tone and begins the meal.

Just as Proverbs 31:28 suggests, the Proverbs 31 passage is used, even today, in Jewish households as a song of praise over the woman of the house. Throughout her life, she steadily walks God's straight path and accepts His correction if she strays to the left or to the right. The strong woman knows God's correction is for the best. It is a blessing. It confirms His presence with her. In turn He offers the Proverbs song in celebration of your strength.

Pause and Reflect

1. What blessings from God do I recognize in my life?

_____

_____

_____

2. How has my obedience to God set me straight, blessed my life, or confirmed His presence with me?

_____

_____

_____

Praying the *Alef-Bet*

Lord, thank You for the blessings of my life. In saying this I recognize Your blessings flow from Your deep love for me and a desire for me to succeed. Even if it means I need to find happiness in You setting me straight so I can continue forward. Lord, I claim peace knowing Your presence hovers over me. Amen.

הָלַל

HALAL

Her children rise up and bless her; her husband also,
and he praises her. —Proverbs 31:28

S ome Sundays were fabulous. The worship team played all her
favorite praise songs, and it was easy to lift her hands and join in
worship. Other Sundays were just okay. But even on those Sundays she noticed others around her with hands and voices lifted high.
That idea stopped her cold. *Wow, God, I'm sorry. I realize praise is not
a style or a favorite song. Please forgive me. I was being selfish. God, I'm
crazy about You. How can I offer You praise today? Here, with no music
or instruments?*

Halal—to Praise

The letters for the Hebrew word for praise, *halal*, hold beautiful imagery. *Halal* in Proverbs 31 is spelled *hei, lamed, lamed. Hei* is a letter that
often represents the spirit of God, and *lamed* is the staff of teaching
and leading. The two *lameds* together appear to be two hands lifted in
praise. Combined, the imagery suggests that to praise, *halal*, is to lead
us to the heart of God, and in response we lift our hands to receive Him.
Halal is the root for the word hallelujah, which means praise God. It's
interesting to note that hallelujah has a plural ending in Hebrew, so
when we praise God, we praise the trinity of God.

Some people consider praise as the time the worship music is playing at church or maybe the time of prayer, but praise takes many forms. It is more than music. We praise with every action of obedience. Our entire life is to reflect praise, more so than you might expect.

Praise, *halal,* is the word used in Proverbs 31:28. It means to make a show, to boast, and be clamorously foolish, a celebration. This is why David danced before the Lord and why Michal thought he was acting like a fool (2 Samuel 6:14, 20). He unabashedly raved and celebrated God. This same type of praise is lavished over the Proverbs woman. It is empowering to be offered this type of praise, but some of us struggle to receive and accept it. Imagine the praise we can offer Christ when we disregard the fear or hesitation we might feel in accepting who we are in Christ and lift our hands in His presence.

Pause and Reflect

1. What is my attitude toward praise?

_____

_____

_____

_____

_____

2. What in my life do I offer as praise?

_____

_____

_____

_____

_____

Praying the *Alef-Bet*

Lord, remind me when I'm just not feeling it that You are still worthy of my praise. Lord, even the quietness of my breathing as I reflect on You is a song of praise as it reaches Your ears. I may not dance before You like David did, but I desire to praise Your name in the midst of all assemblies (Psalm 22:22). Give me courage and freedom to do so. Amen.

RESH

Many daughters have done nobly, but you excel them all.
—Proverbs 31:29

F atigue was taking a toll. Jennifer gladly wrangled the kids to school. Prepping lunches and taking her turn in the carpool on the way to work was a common routine. But when you add the mounds of insurance paperwork, navigating the VA benefits, and getting her husband to physical therapy to the ever-growing grocery list, laundry pile, and activity calendar . . . nothing was ever all taken care of. She thanked God daily her husband's deployment was over. He was alive, but he wasn't whole. Not physically, not mentally, not yet. Healing takes time.

Lord, I know this is a season of sacrifice. I pray I can be the wife he needs.

She lingered a bit longer, savoring the quiet moment. Eyeing the stack of paperwork, she inhaled deeply and picked up her reading glasses.

Resh—the Head, First in Rank

Proverbs 31:29 continues the well-deserved honor over the strong woman. "Many daughters have done nobly, but you excel them all." Does that description remind you of verse 10 ("An excellent wife, who can find?")? Nobly, in verse 29, and excellent, in verse 10, is the same word for strong, *chayil*. The poem begins and ends with an acknowledgement of this woman's strength.

The imagery for *resh* is the head, as relates to the head of the line and the most important. In Hebrew, the first word in this verse is *rab*, which means abundant rank and quality. *Resh* shows this woman has priority or is first over many.

Another word in the verse, *alah*, or excel, is an interesting word. Its Hebrew root means to go up, to ascend, but it references the ascending smoke from a burnt offering or sacrifice. The husband acknowledges the worth of the strong woman rises above others. The word choice links her praise to an acknowledgement of her strength and the sacrifices she makes.

Women, wives, and moms often sacrifice for others. I sacrifice for my family, knowing it will likely go unnoticed. To have my family's acknowledgment and appreciation is high praise indeed. Knowing my actions please God and become a fragrant aroma rising to Him, above all else, makes it even sweeter (Philippians 4:18).

Pause and Reflect

1. What sacrifices have I made for others?

_____

_____

_____

_____

2. Are they done begrudgingly, out of obligation, or with the idea it is a sacrifice for God?

_____

_____

_____

_____

Praying the *Alef-Bet*

Lord, I pray I have a spirit of service toward others. My desire is not to draw accolades but to offer myself as a living sacrifice so all I do rises to You as a fragrant offering. Amen.

SHIN

Charm is deceitful and beauty is vain, but a woman
who fears the LORD, she shall be praised. —Proverbs 31:30

*W*ow, time flies, she thought as she walked through the park
with her husband. Linda gave his hand a squeeze.

"What was that for?" he asked nonchalantly.

"Oh, just reminiscing. Our twenty-fifth wedding anniversary is
coming up." Linda released his hand and slipped her arm through his.

"We've come a long way, baby." He patted her hand and laughed.

"We have." She paused. "Back then, in the thick of things, did you
ever think we'd make it this long?"

He knew she was referring to those troubled, turbulent times in their
marriage. "I wasn't certain, but I was sure of our commitment to each
other and to Christ. We have been through some fire. They were fires
of refinement not destruction. God is good."

"Yes, He is." She leaned her head on his shoulder and walked with
him, enjoying the peace.

Shin—the Teeth, Fire, to Destroy

Shin has the imagery of healthy, firmly rooted teeth and a secondary
picture of fire. The imagery links the letter to destruction and devour.
Both teeth and fire can consume and destroy, but they can also be agents
of change. Fire is often a symbol for God and His passion for us. *Shin*

can also represent God's unlimited *shalom*, His peace in the midst of those destructive fires. God of *shalom*, unlimited peace.

The Hebrew word for charm, *chen*, begins this verse. It is described as a fleeting deception or a sham, like a smoke screen. It means favor or grace, but unlike the perfect, never-ending grace of Christ, the grace we offer can be limited and dependent on our mood. It can fade away like a vapor. The strong woman is praised for her steadfast, unchanging dedication and fear of the Lord.

Grace is a result of God's consuming love for us, and it too can be transforming. His passion for us can burn away the destructive influences in our life and firmly root us in peace.

Pause and Reflect

1. What destroys my peace? How can God's unmerited grace transform the times I am not at peace?

2. What does fear of the Lord look like in my life?

Praying the *Alef-Bet*

Lord, there are times in my life when I feel as though I am facing a firestorm. You, Lord, offer unending grace, and that brings me peace. Father, I pray my dedication to You remains firmly rooted in respect for You. Amen.

YARE

The fear of the Lord is the beginning of knowledge;
fools despise wisdom and instruction. —Proverbs 1:7

A bigail had heard the stories of this man—God's anointed but not yet king. Her husband was foolish. Her thoughts did not disparage him. His name, Nabal, meant foolish, and his actions revealed he embraced his name. By rejecting David's plea for food and drink, Nabal foolishly rejected God. And now Abigail trotted her donkey along the path leading down from the mountain. It was not wise to disregard God's instruction. With God's blessing, she would meet David and intercede for her husband's life.

David and his men approached as Abigail hurried to dismount. She fell on her face before him. "Please forgive my transgressions. You are fighting on behalf of the Lord. May your house endure. When the Lord does for you according to all He has spoken, please remember me."

David squatted low and lifted her face. Looking into her eyes he responded, "Blessed be the Lord who has sent you. You have tasted and perceived with wisdom, and it has kept me from bloodshed" (a summary of 1 Samuel 25:28–32).

Yare—Fear

We are nearing the end of this rich Proverbs 31 passage and the devotions. I pray the previous twenty-nine days have revealed a new understanding of the Proverbs 31 Woman. She is truly a woman of strength. Much has been said about this woman, and she deserves to be acknowledged and praised. Throughout the passage, her strength is noted six times, and her wisdom and insight five times. But her fear of the Lord is only mentioned once. Once is enough.

This *yare*, this fear, is not used to intimidate or control. Fear of the Lord understands His holiness and the depth of His love for you. It is a desire to honor God so much you dread disappointing Him. You have tasted God's goodness, and nothing else will satisfy. Revelation 15 records the victorious singing of God's marvelous works and righteous ways. These victorious believers acknowledge that the earth will glorify Him in fear as an act of praise. This fear is for your protection. It is not to hold you captive in bondage. In Christ, we are free indeed.

The first chapter of Proverbs contains the phrase, "The fear of the LORD is the beginning of knowledge" (Proverbs 1:7). Proverbs ends with the same message in Proverbs 31:30. It is a blessing for the woman of strength because she realizes the wisdom of revering God with a holy fear.

Pause and Reflect

1. As a believer in Jesus Christ, what do I consider my crowning achievement?

2. How is fear of the Lord revealed in my life?

_____

_____

_____

_____

_____

_____

Praying the *Alef-Bet*

Lord, I desire to completely honor You in every aspect of my life, in thought, word, and deed. Above all I would like to be recognized as a woman of strength who fears You. Not because You demand my affection and obedience (though that would be enough reason alone) but because in my love for You I recognize Your boundaries as my protection and wisdom for an abundant life. Amen.

TAV

Give her the product of her hands,
and let her works praise her in the gates.
—Proverbs 31:31

T o be honest, she wasn't looking forward to attending the women's retreat. The weekend's theme was renewal, and she didn't miss the irony of the timing at the end of a busy, tiring week. Was renewal even possible? Convinced God would never use her for anything important, she felt defeated before setting foot in the building. *My sin is too great. I've made far too many mistakes. If any of these people knew my truth, I'd be asked to leave.*

The speakers had a much different message. It contained the truth of God's Word.

Tav—the Cross, the Mark

The final letter in the Hebrew alphabet is *tav*. Its word picture is a cross, and it relates to a sign and making a mark, like X marks the spot. Road signs direct us, and hazard signs warn us. We've grown to depend on signs and the accuracy of their messages. With this in mind, we can understand how *tav* represents truth.

Proverbs 31:31 begins by appointing a reward to the woman of strength. Her faithful, rich life designates this woman as worthy of praise at the city gates. She is not only to be quietly affirmed in the privacy of her home but boasted over at the busiest place in town. The same place her husband is esteemed.

A modern understanding of this passage suggests she is deserving because of her perfection. Her feathers are never ruffled, and she glides through life with ease and noble behavior. The Hebrew language reveals the truth of her reality. Women of strength face spiritual warfare and crossroads in life. They embrace their authority and are alert watchmen. They are strong warriors who diligently commit their ways to Christ, seeking His direction and support. They leave a mark. God acknowledges your struggles in life and praises your victory—from A to Z.

Pause and Reflect

1. Which Proverbs woman do I best relate to? Would I describe myself as the dignified woman of excellence, a woman of honor, which we've come to understand Proverbs 31 represents? Or do I better represent the warrior woman of strength?

_____

_____

_____

2. What legacy would I like to leave?

_____

_____

_____

Praying the *Alef-Bet*

Lord, You died on the Cross for me, the final sign of grace and redemption. Thank You, Father, that sin does not have the final word. I pray the legacy I leave here on earth points others to You as I live and walk in the blessings of Your truth. Amen.

**If you enjoyed this book, will you consider sharing
the message with others?**

Let us know your thoughts at info@ironstreammedia.com.
You can also let the author know by visiting or sharing a photo
of the cover on our social media pages or leaving a review
at a retailer's site. All of it helps us get the message out!

Facebook.com/IronStreamMedia

―――――――

Ascender Books, New Hope® Publishers, Iron Stream Books,
and New Hope Kidz are imprints of Iron Stream Media,
which derives its name from Proverbs 27:17,
"As iron sharpens iron, so one person sharpens another."

This sharpening describes the process of discipleship,
one to another. With this in mind, Iron Stream Media provides
a variety of solutions for churches, ministry leaders, and nonprofits ranging
from in-depth Bible study curriculum and Christian book publishing to
custom publishing and consultative services.
Through our popular Life Bible Study, Student Life Bible Study brands, and
New Hope imprints, ISM provides web-based full-year
and short-term Bible study teaching plans as well as printed devotionals,
Bibles, and discipleship curriculum.

For more information on ISM and Ascender Books, please visit

IronStreamMedia.com

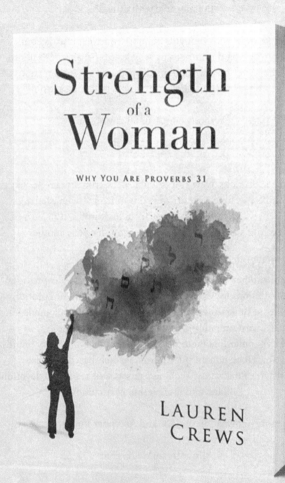